Quick &

No-Bake
Cookbook

Over 75 delicious recipes for cookies, cakes, pies, and other tasty treats!

By Susan Evans

Free Bonus!

Would you like to receive one of my cookbooks for free? Just leave me on honest review on Amazon and I will send you a digital version of the cookbook of your choice! All you have to do is email me proof of your review and the desired cookbook and format to susan.evans.author@gmail.com. Thank you for your support, and have fun cooking!

CAKES AND PIES 31

FRUIT DESSERTS 53

OTHER TREATS......67

THANK YOU......87

INTRODUCTION

Everyone loves desserts, but sometimes it's just too hot to turn on the oven or we don't have the time to deal with the preparation baking requires. Furthermore, baking recipes can be intimidating for less experienced chefs. If your baking abilities prevent you from attempting delicious treats, let your fears of ruining a dessert go, and create some deliciously easy no-bake desserts! The following tasty recipes render preparing home-made treats simple and quick for everyone, from the busy mother to novice chef.

This no-bake cookbook contains everything you need to make perfect desserts that will make everyone's mouth water. Impress your family and guests by presenting the perfect finish to a meal: a decadent dessert that requires no oven! From cookies, to cakes, to pies, to fudge, to dessert bars, and other treats; there's something here for everyone to enjoy! So let's turn off that oven and let's get cooking!

MEASUREMENT CONVERSIONS

Liquid/Volume Measurements (approximate)

1 teaspoon = 1/6 fluid ounce (oz.) = 1/3 tablespoon = 5 ml

1 tablespoon = 1/2 fluid ounce (oz.) = 3 teaspoons = 15 ml

1 fluid ounce (oz.) = 2 tablespoons = 1/8 cup = 30 ml

1/4 cup = 2 fluid ounces (oz.) = 4 tablespoons = 60 ml

1/3 cup = 2⅔ fluid ounces (oz.) = 5 ⅓ tablespoons = 80 ml

1/2 cup = 4 fluid ounces (oz.) = 8 tablespoons = 120 ml

2/3 cup = 5⅓ fluid ounces (oz.) = 10⅔ tablespoons = 160 ml

3/4 cup = 6 fluid ounces (oz.) = 12 tablespoons = 180 ml

7/8 cup = 7 fluid ounces (oz.) = 14 tablespoons = 210 ml

1 cup = 8 fluid ounces (oz.) = 1/2 pint = 240 ml

1 pint = 16 fluid ounces (oz.) = 2 cups = 1/2 quart = 475 ml

1 quart = 4 cups = 32 fluid ounces (oz.) = 2 pints = 950 ml

1 liter = 1.055 quarts = 4.22 cups = 2.11 pints = 1000 ml

1 gallon = 4 quarts = 8 pints = 3.8 liters

Dry/Weight Measurements (approximate)

1 ounce (oz.) = 30 grams (g)

2 ounces (oz.) = 55 grams (g)

3 ounces (oz.) = 85 grams (g)

1/4 pound (lb.) = 4 ounces (oz.) = 125 grams (g)

1/2 pound (lb.) = 8 ounces (oz.) = 240 grams (g)

3/4 pound (lb.) = 12 ounces (oz.) = 375 grams (g)

1 pound (lb.) = 16 ounces (oz.) = 455 grams (g)

2 pounds (lbs.) = 32 ounces (oz.) = 910 grams (g)

1 kilogram (kg) = 2.2 pounds (lbs.) = 1000 gram (g)

COOKIES, BARS, AND TRUFFLES

Chocolate Truffles

SERVINGS: 20-30
PREP TIME: 15 min.
TOTAL TIME: 45 min.

Ingredients

- 1 package Oreos or other chocolate sandwich cookies
- 1 (8 oz.) package cream cheese, cut into ½ inch cubes
- 8 oz. semi-sweet chocolate, melted
- ¼ cup white chocolate, melted

Instructions

1. In a food processor, pulse cookies until finely ground. Transfer into a large plastic food storage bag. Add cream cheese to the bag, and close. Shake to coat the cream cheese with the cookies and massage to squash cream cheese pieces and incorporate the cookies.
2. Roll the cookie-cream cheese mixture into 2″ balls. Dip balls in the semi-sweet chocolate, remove and shake off the excess. Place on a baking sheet lined with foil or parchment paper.
3. Dip with a fork into the white chocolate, and shake it over the dipped chocolate truffles to decorate.
4. Refrigerate balls for at least 30 minutes to an hour before serving.

Oatmeal Cookie Balls

SERVINGS: 24
PREP TIME: 10 min.
TOTAL TIME: 30 min.

Ingredients

- 2 cups rolled oats
- ¾ cup white sugar
- 3 tablespoons unsweetened cocoa powder
- 1 tablespoon water
- ½ teaspoon vanilla
- ½ cup butter, softened
- 2 tablespoons peanut butter
- 1 cup confectioners' sugar

Instructions

1. In a large bowl, combine oats, sugar and cocoa. Mix in water, vanilla, butter and peanut butter to form a dough.
2. Roll dough into balls 1 to 2 inches in diameter.
3. Roll balls in confectioners' sugar until thickly coated.
4. Chill 20 minutes before serving.

Peanut Butter Cookie Dough Bars

SERVINGS: 64
PREP/TOTAL TIME: 15 min. + refrigeration

Ingredients

- ½ cup unsalted butter, softened
- ¾ cup light brown sugar, packed
- 1 teaspoon pure vanilla extract
- ¼ cup creamy peanut butter
- 2 cup all-purpose flour
- 1 can (14 oz.) sweetened condensed milk
- 2 cup mini chocolate chip morsels
- ¾ cup creamy peanut butter
- ¾ cup semi-sweet chocolate chip morsels

Instructions

1. In a large mixing bowl, beat softened butter with brown sugar until combined. Add vanilla and peanut butter, beat until fluffy. Add flour and sweetened condensed milk. Beat until everything is well blended. Fold in the mini chocolate chip morsels.
2. Press into an 8 x 8 inch baking dish.
3. In a microwave safe medium sized bowl, add peanut butter and chocolate chips for the frosting. Melt for one minute. Stir and spread over the cookie dough.
4. Refrigerate for 3 hours or overnight. Cut into bite sized pieces.

Pumpkin Spice Nanaimo Bars

SERVINGS: 9
PREP/TOTAL TIME: 30 min. + refrigeration

Ingredients

- ½ cup butter
- ⅓ cup cocoa powder
- ¼ cup sugar
- 1 egg
- 1¼ cup graham cracker crumbs
- 1 cup shredded coconut
- ¼ cup finely chopped pecans
- ¼ cup butter
- 1 box (3.4 oz.) pumpkin spice pudding mix
- ¼ cup milk
- 1¼ cups powdered sugar
- 4-5 oz. chocolate (or ¾ cup chocolate chips)
- 1 tablespoon butter

Instructions

1. Melt butter in a saucepan over low heat. Add cocoa and sugar, and quickly stir to combine.
2. Add egg before mixture becomes too hot, and mix well. Continue cooking and stirring another minute to let mixture thicken. Remove from heat.
3. Stir in cracker crumbs, coconut, and nuts. Press mixture into the bottom of a 9x9 inch pan, and let chill while you make the filling.
4. Soften butter and combine with pudding, milk and powdered sugar. Beat until smooth. Spread evenly over crust layer.
5. Melt chocolate and butter in the microwave, in 30-second intervals, stirring between each. Quickly pour over other layers, and smooth with a knife.
6. Let bars chill for at least 1 hour before cutting into bars.
7. Keep in refrigerator, and serve chilled.

S'mores Cereal Bars

SERVINGS: 6-8
PREP/TOTAL TIME: 30 min.

Ingredients

- ¼ cup butter
- 3 ¼ cups mini marshmallows, divided
- 4 cups Golden Grahams cereal
- ½ cup milk chocolate chips

Instructions

1. Line an 8x8 inch pan with foil then lightly spray with non-stick cooking spray.
2. In a 3 quart saucepan, melt butter over medium heat. Add 3 cups marshmallows reserving ¼ cup marshmallows for topping. Continue to cook, stirring until all marshmallows have melted. Remove from heat and stir in cereal.
3. Transfer cereal mixture to prepared 8x8 pan. While still warm, top with remaining marshmallows and chocolate chips.
4. Let cool completely. Remove bars from pan, remove foil and cut into squares.

Peanut Butter Puffs Bars

SERVINGS: 16
PREP/TOTAL TIME: 10 min.

Ingredients

- 3 tablespoons butter
- 1 (10 oz.) package large marshmallows
- ½ cup peanut butter
- 7 cups Reese's Peanut Butter Puffs Cereal
- 1 cup peanut butter cups, chopped
- ½ cup peanut butter candies

Instructions

1. Spray a 9x13 in pan with non-stick spray.
2. Melt together butter, marshmallows, and peanut butter in a large pot until smooth. Mix in cereal until well coated. Add peanut butter cups and candies and mix to incorporate.
3. Pour into prepared pan, and use a spatula to press down evenly.
4. Let cool completely before cutting into squares.

Double Shot Cookies

SERVINGS: 10
PREP TIME: 10 min.
TOTAL TIME: 30 min.

Ingredients

- 2 cup granulated sugar
- ¼ cup unsweetened cocoa powder
- ½ teaspoons espresso powder
- ½ cup milk
- ½ cup unsalted butter
- pinch of kosher salt
- ½ cup JIF Mocha Cappuccino Hazelnut Spread
- 3 cup quick oats

Instructions

1. Cook sugar, cocoa, espresso powder, milk and butter over medium heat. Bring to a boil and boil for 1 minute. Remove from heat. Add and stir in salt, Jif spread and oats.
2. Drop by the teaspoonful on parchment paper and cool.
3. Refrigerate.

Chocolate Peanut Butter Cracker Bars

SERVINGS: 5 slices
PREP TIME: 15 min.
TOTAL TIME: 25 min.

Ingredients

- ¾ cup butter, room temperature
- 1¼ cup smooth peanut butter, divided
- 3 cups crushed crackers (about 2 ½ sleeves Ritz)
- 2 cups mini chocolate chips, divided

Instructions

1. In a mixing bowl, combine 1 cup peanut butter and butter, blending until smooth and creamy. Stir in crushed crackers and ½ cup mini chocolate chips. Press peanut butter mix into the bottom of a greased 9x13 inch pan.
2. In a small sauce pan over low heat, melt remaining chocolate chips with ¼ cup peanut butter until smooth.
3. Spread melted chocolate evenly over peanut butter mixture. Refrigerate until set, at least 1 hour.
4. Cut into bars and serve.

Chocolate Chip Peanut Butter Cheesecake Bars

SERVINGS: 16
PREP TIME: 15 min.
TOTAL TIME: 35 min.

Ingredients

- 1 cup crushed chocolate wafer cookies
- 4 tablespoons melted butter
- ½ teaspoon gelatin
- 8 oz. room-temperature cream cheese
- 7 oz. sweetened condensed milk
- ¼ cup peanut butter
- ½ cup mini chocolate chips

Instructions

1. Mix together cookie crumbs and melted butter. Press into the bottom of an 8×8 inch baking dish. Set aside.
2. In a small bowl, combine gelatin with 1 tablespoon of water. Let sit for 5 minutes.
3. In another bowl, beat cream cheese, sweetened condensed milk and peanut butter together until smooth. Microwave gelatin for 10 seconds to melt, then beat into the cream cheese mixture. Stir in the chocolate chips. Gently spread the mixture over the crumb crust.
4. Freeze for 20 minutes then cut into squares.

Coconut Truffles

SERVINGS: 50
PREP TIME: 15 min.
TOTAL TIME: 20 min.

Ingredients

- 8 oz. cream cheese, softened
- ½ teaspoons coconut extract (or almond extract)
- 5 cups powdered sugar
- 2-3 cups coconut flakes

Instructions

1. Mix together softened cream cheese with extract. Add powdered sugar and ½ cup coconut to cream cheese mix a bit at a time, beating until smooth.
2. Form balls of the truffle mix and roll them in coconut. Place on a sheet pan.
3. Chill for 10-15 minutes before serving.

Chocolate Peanut Butter Krispie Cheesecake Bars

SERVINGS: 24
PREP/TOTAL TIME: 30 min. + refrigeration

Ingredients

For the Crust:
- 1 cup milk chocolate chips
- 2 tablespoons milk
- ¼ cup peanut butter
- 3 tablespoons honey
- 3 cups Krispie rice cereal

For the filling:
- 1 (8 oz.) package of reduced-fat cream cheese, softened
- ½ cup peanut butter
- ¼ cup granulated sugar
- 1 (8 oz.) package of light whipped topping, thawed.

Topping:
- ¼ cup peanut butter
- ½ tablespoons granulated sugar
- melted chocolate, or chocolate syrup, for drizzling (optional)

Instructions

1. Line a 9x13 inch baking dish with parchment paper and set aside.
2. In a large bowl, combine chocolate chips and milk. Melt on half power in the microwave using 20 second intervals, stirring between each interval, until the chocolate is smooth and melted.
3. Stir in the peanut butter and honey until the peanut butter is melted and mixed in,
4. Stir in the rice cereal until well coated.
5. Pat crust into bottom of the prepared pan. Set aside.
6. Beat in the sugar until well incorporated.
7. Fold in the whipped topping until well mixed in and then pour the cheesecake mixture over top of the crust. Spread out evenly.

8. Melt the peanut butter in the microwave, and stir in the granulated sugar,
9. Drizzle over the cheesecake layer and swirl with a toothpick or chopstick.
10. Freeze for at least 4 hours.
11. Let the bars thaw for 5 minutes before lifting out of the pan and slicing with knife.
12. Drizzle with melted chocolate or chocolate syrup, if desired.

Nutella S'mores Granola Bars

SERVINGS: 10 bars
PREP/TOTAL TIME: 15 min.

Ingredients

- ¼ cup butter
- ¼ cup honey
- ¼ cup Nutella spread
- 2½ cups rolled oats
- ½ cup miniature chocolate chips
- ½ cup miniature marshmallow bits

Instructions

1. In a saucepan over medium-low heat stir butter and honey until melted. Add and stir in the Nutella spread until melted. Pour in oats and stir until completely coated. Let cool 5 minutes.
2. Add mini chocolate chips and mini marshmallow bits. Stir gently until mixed. Press firmly into a greased 8x8 inch baking dish. Let set.
3. Cut into 10 bars and serve.

Chocolate Pumpkin Coco Bars

SERVINGS: 8
PREP TIME: 20 min.
TOTAL TIME: 40 min.

Ingredients

- 10 medjool dates, pitted and soaked for 15-30 minutes in water
- 1 cup almonds
- 1½ tablespoon dark, unsweetened cocoa powder
- 1½ teaspoon cinnamon, divided
- ¼ cup coconut butter, softened until spreadable
- 1 banana
- ¼ cup pumpkin puree
- 2 tablespoons honey
- unsweetened coconut flakes for garnish (optional)

Instructions

1. Combine dates, almonds, cocoa powder and ½ teaspoon cinnamon in a food processor. Process until a ball starts to form and dough is sticky.
2. Transfer to a 9×5 inch baking pan or a bread loaf pan and spread/flatten out across the bottom of the entire pan.
3. Spread softened coconut butter as evenly as possible on top of the date/nut mixture.
4. Add banana, pumpkin, honey and remaining cinnamon to the food processor and process until smooth and fully mixed.
5. Pour mixture on top of the coconut butter, spreading evenly across the entire surface.
6. Sprinkle coconut flakes on top and freeze until set, around 30 minutes.
7. Cut into 8 squares once frozen.

Chocolate Peanut Butter Granola Bars

SERVINGS: 8-10 bars
PREP/TOTAL TIME: 15 min. + refrigeration

Ingredients

- 1 cup peanut butter
- ½ cup honey
- ½ cup + 1 teaspoon coconut oil, divided
- 2¾ cups old fashioned rolled oats
- ¾ cup chopped peanuts
- ¼ cup mini chocolate chips
- ⅓ cup semi-sweet chocolate chips

Instructions

1. Line a 9-inch square baking dish with parchment paper. Set aside.
2. Combine peanut butter, honey, and ½ cup coconut oil in a medium pot over low heat. Stir until smooth and completely melted. Remove from heat and stir in oats and peanuts.
3. Pour mixture into baking dish. Spread an even layer and pressing down firmly with the back of a spatula. Refrigerate for 10 minutes or until cool. Remove from fridge and sprinkle mini chocolate chips over the top, pressing down lightly with the back of a spoon to set in granola. Place in refrigerator and chill 2 hours or until firm. Slice into small bars and remove from pan.
4. Melt semi-sweet chocolate chips and one teaspoon coconut oil in a heatproof bowl over a pot of simmering water. Drizzle melted chocolate over bars and let set.
5. Store granola bars in an airtight container in the refrigerator with wax paper separating the layers.

Peanut Butter Cheesecake Bars

SERVINGS: 8
PREP TIME: 5 min.
TOTAL TIME: 25 min.

Ingredients

- 1½ cup crushed chocolate Teddy Grahams
- 4 tablespoons melted butter
- 1 packet unflavored gelatin
- 8 oz. room-temperature cream cheese
- 7 oz. (½ can) sweetened condensed milk
- ½ cup peanut butter
- ½ cup milk chocolate chips

Instructions

1. Crush the Teddy Grahams in a zip-lock bag. Mix together the cookie crumbs and the melted butter and press firmly into the bottom of an 8×8 inch baking dish. Set aside.
2. In a small bowl, combine gelatin with 1 tablespoon of water. Let sit for 5 minutes until firm.
3. In a medium sized bowl, beat together the cream cheese, sweetened condensed milk and peanut butter until smooth. Microwave the gelatin for 10 seconds to melt, then beat into the cream cheese mixture. Stir in the chocolate chips. Gently spread the mixture over the crumb crust.
4. Freeze for 20 minutes then cut into squares.

White Chocolate Frito Bars

Ingredients

- 2 (10.25 oz.) bags Frito Scoops
- 2 cup sugar
- 2 cup light corn syrup
- 1 teaspoon vanilla
- 2½ cup peanut butter
- 2 squares vanilla CandiQuik

Instructions

1. Pour Frito Scoops into a gallon Ziploc bag. Crush until they are large pieces. Pour into a large bowl.
2. In a medium saucepan, combine sugar and white syrup. Bring to a boil and boil for 1 minute. Remove from heat and add peanut butter and vanilla. Stir until peanut butter has melted and is combined.
3. Pour over Frito's and mix well. Pour mix into a greased jelly roll pan.
4. Melt CandiQuik according to package directions. Drizzle over bars.

Fun-fetti Cookie Dough Bars

SERVINGS: 10
PREP TIME: 20 min. + refrigeration

Ingredients

- ½ cup butter, at room temperature
- ½ cup white sugar
- 1 teaspoon vanilla extract
- 1 (14 oz.) can sweetened condensed milk
- ⅛ teaspoon salt
- 1 cup yellow cake mix, dry
- 1 and ⅓ cup flour, spoon and level
- 2 cups (1 bag) white chocolate chips, separated
- ⅓ cup + 4 tablespoons sprinkles, separated
- ½ teaspoon vegetable oil

Instructions

1. Line an 8x8 inch baking pan with parchment paper.
2. In a medium sized bowl, using hand mixers, mix together the butter, white sugar, and vanilla extract until light and creamy. Beat in the sweetened condensed milk until completely combined. Mix in the salt, yellow cake mix, and flour. Beat until completely combined. If it is still sticky, add more flour.
3. Using a wooden spoon, stir in one cup of white chocolate chips and ⅓ cup of sprinkles. Press the mixture into the lined 8x8 inch baking pan.
4. In a small microwave safe bowl, combined 1 cup white chocolate chips with ½ teaspoon vegetable oil. Microwave in bursts of 30 seconds, stirring in between the bursts for 15-20 seconds.
5. Using a spatula spread the white chocolate evenly over the bars. Sprinkle the remaining sprinkles (more or less if desired) over the white chocolate. Allow to harden and leave in the fridge for at least 3 hours.

Peanut Butter Bars

SERVINGS: 8
PREP TIME: 5 min.
TOTAL TIME: 1 hour

Ingredients

- 1 cup butter melted
- 2 cups graham cracker crumbs (use the boxed kind, or grind them in a food processor)
- 2 cups confectioners' sugar (powdered sugar)
- 1 cup + 4 tablespoons peanut butter
- 1½ cups milk chocolate chips

Instructions

1. In a medium bowl, mix the melted butter, graham cracker crumbs, confectioners' sugar, and 1 cup peanut butter until well combined. Press evenly into the bottom of an ungreased 9×13 inch pan.
2. In a microwave, melt the chips with the peanut butter, stirring every 30 seconds until melted and smooth. Spread over the peanut butter layer.
3. Refrigerate for at least one hour before cutting into squares. Serve.

Peanut Butter Corn Flake Cookies

SERVINGS: 20
PREP TIME: 5 min.
TOTAL TIME: 15 min.

Ingredients

- 1 cup sugar
- 1 cup light corn syrup
- 1 cup creamy peanut butter
- 6 cup Corn Flakes cereal

Instructions

1. Heat sugar and syrup in a small saucepan, until the sugar dissolves. Do not boil. Remove from heat and stir in the peanut butter.
2. Put Corn Flakes in a large bowl and pour sugary mixture over them. Gently mix everything until coated, being careful not to smash up Corn Flakes.
3. Drop onto wax paper by the spoonful. Let them cool and set for a few minutes.

Bird Egg Nest Chocolate Cookies

SERVINGS: 4
PREP/TOTAL TIME: 15 min.

Ingredients

- 1 (11-12 oz.) bag milk chocolate chips
- 1 (11-12 oz.) bag butterscotch chips
- 1 (10-12 oz.) bag Chow Mein noodles
- M&M's, Jellybeans, Chocolate eggs, or any "egg-shaped" candy

Instructions

1. Place the two bags of chips into a microwave-safe bowl. Melt in microwave on 50% power for 60 seconds. Stir and repeat until all chips are smoothly melted.
2. Add bag of chow Mein noodles to the melted chocolate and stir until noodles are coated.
3. Lay out wax paper and drop a large tablespoonful of chocolate noodles onto wax paper. Mold into a "bird nest" shape.
4. Place a couple of "egg" candies on top of the chocolate nest. Let harden and place in the fridge.

Peppermint Cathedral Fudge Cookies

SERVINGS: 12
PREP/TOTAL TIME: 30 min. + freezing

Ingredients

- 1 cup semisweet chocolate chips
- 2 tablespoons butter
- 1 egg
- 3 cups mini peppermint marshmallows
- 1 cup white chocolate peppermint M&Ms, chopped

Instructions

1. Melt together chocolate chips and butter over low heat in a heavy medium saucepan. Place egg in a small bowl and add some of the chocolate mixture. Return the mix to the saucepan and cook over low heat for 2 minutes, making sure to whisk often. Remove from heat and pour into a heatproof bowl. Cool for 15 minutes. Stir in marshmallows and ½ cup M&Ms. Chill in bowl for 30 minutes.
2. On a sheet of parchment paper, shape the chocolate mixture into a log, 1½ inches in diameter. Sprinkle and press remaining ½ cup M&Ms into the top and sides until they stick. Wrap up tightly and twist ends of paper to seal.
3. Freeze for 4 hours or overnight. Remove from paper and cut into slices.
4. Keep stored in the refrigerator.

Peanut Butter Chocolate Chip Cheesecake Bars

SERVINGS: 16
PREP TIME: 15 min.
TOTAL TIME: 35 min.

Ingredients

- 1 cup crushed chocolate wafer cookies
- 4 tablespoons melted butter
- ½ teaspoon gelatin
- 8 oz. room-temperature cream cheese
- 7 oz. sweetened condensed milk
- ¼ cup peanut butter
- ½ cup mini chocolate chips

Instructions

1. Mix together cookie crumbs and the melted butter. Press into the bottom of an 8×8 inch baking dish. Set aside.
2. Combine gelatin with 1 tablespoon of water in a small bowl. Let sit for 5 minutes.
3. In a different bowl, beat together the cream cheese, sweetened condensed milk and peanut butter until smooth. Microwave the gelatin for 10 seconds to melt, then beat into the cream cheese mixture. Stir in chocolate chips. Spread the mixture over the crumb crust.
4. Freeze for 20 minutes.
5. Cut into squares and serve.

5. No-Egg Vanilla Cookies

Ingredients

- 1½ cups flour
- 1/4 cup milk
- 1 teaspoon vinegar
- 1 cup butter
- 1/2 cup powdered sugar
- 1 teaspoon vanilla essence

Instructions

1. Mix flour, milk, vinegar, butter, sugar and vanilla.
2. Knead flour and make a smooth dough.
3. Create 24 small balls and flatten them with a fork.
4. Place six at a time on a microwave baking tray or lightly greased greaseproof paper. Microwave for 1½ – 2 ¼ minutes. Give the tray a half turn halfway through.
5. Remove and allow to cool.
6. Repeat with the remaining batches.

Circus Animals and Cookie Dough Truffle Bars

SERVINGS: 8-10 bars
PREP/TOTAL TIME: 30 min. + refrigeration

Ingredients

- 1½ cup Circus Animal cookies
- 1 cup unsalted butter (2 sticks), softened
- 1 cup granulated sugar
- ¾ cup light brown sugar
- 2¼ cup all-purpose flour
- ½ teaspoons salt
- 3 tablespoons milk
- 1 tablespoon pure vanilla extract
- ¼ cup sprinkles
- 12 oz. white chocolate chips
- ¼ cup heavy cream
- ¼ cup sprinkles

Instructions

1. Place Circus Animal cookies into a large Ziploc bag. Gently crush cookies into small pieces with a rolling pin to create a mix of crumbs and cookie chunks.
2. In a medium-sized bowl, combine butter and both sugars. Mix with a mixer until smooth. Add flour and salt. Mix just until combined and crumbly.
3. Add vanilla extract and milk. Mix until dough is soft. Add crushed cookies and sprinkles.
4. Line a 9x9-inch pan with parchment paper or foil, and wrap over top edge. Empty cookie dough into pan and gently press dough into the pan with your fingers.
5. In a microwave safe bowl, combine chocolate chips with heavy cream. Microwave on high for 90 seconds. Remove and whisk until chocolate begins to melt.
6. Pour melted chocolate over top of cookie dough. Top with additional sprinkles.

7. Leave on the counter for at least 30 minutes and allow chocolate to cool. Refrigerate until firm.
8. Remove from refrigerator 20 minutes before serving.
9. Lift parchment paper out and cut bars into squares.

Nutella Cookies

SERVINGS: 20 slices
PREP TIME: 5 min.
TOTAL TIME: 15 min.

Ingredients

- 2 cup sugar
- ¼ cup cocoa
- ½ cup milk
- ½ cup margarine
- 1 teaspoon vanilla
- pinch of salt
- ¼ cup peanut butter
- ¼ cup Nutella
- 3 cup quick oats

Instructions

1. Cook sugar, cocoa, milk and margarine over medium heat. Boil one minute and then remove from heat.
2. Stir in vanilla, salt, peanut butter, Nutella and oats until combined.
3. Drop mix by teaspoon on wax paper and cool.
4. Refrigerate.

CAKES AND PIES

Vanilla Bean Cheesecake Blueberry Pie

SERVINGS: 2 servings
PREP/TOTAL TIME: 25 min.

Ingredients

- 1 cup heavy cream
- 1 (8-oz.) package cream cheese, at room temperature
- ½ cup sugar
- 1 vanilla bean, seeds scraped
- 1 cup graham cracker crumbs
- 1 (20-oz.) can blueberry pie filling

Instructions

1. Whip heavy cream in the bowl of an electric mixer with the whisk attachment, until stiff peaks form. Set aside.
2. In a clean bowl of an electric mixer fitted with a paddle attachment, beat cream cheese, sugar and vanilla bean seeds until smooth. Scrape the sides of the bowl and beaters as needed. Fold in ⅓ of the whipped cream to lighten it. Then add remaining whipped cream, gently folding until the filling is light and fluffy.
3. Using 2 mason jars, pour the filling into each glass, layering with the graham cracker crumbs and blueberry pie filling.
4. Serve chilled.

Strawberry Eclair Cake

SERVINGS: 15
PREP TIME: 15 min.
TOTAL TIME: 2 hours

Ingredients

For the Cake:

- 1 box (14.4 oz.) Graham Crackers
- 2 pkg. (1 oz. each) Sugar Free Cheesecake Pudding mix
- 2½ cup skim milk
- 12 oz. Fat Free Cool Whip, thawed
- 1 pint fresh strawberries, hulled and sliced

For the Frosting:

- 2 oz. unsweetened baking chocolate, melted
- 2 teaspoons light corn syrup
- 1 teaspoon vanilla extract
- 3 tablespoons unsalted butter, melted
- 1 ½ cup powdered sugar
- 2 tablespoons milk

Instructions

1. Mix pudding mix with milk using a whisk. Beat for 2 minutes by hand. Fold in Cool Whip and set aside.
2. Layer a 13x9 baking dish with a layer of graham crackers. Top with half of pudding mix. Lay half of sliced strawberries on top of pudding. Repeat the layers with Graham crackers, remaining pudding and remaining strawberries. Top with one more layer of Graham crackers.
3. For the frosting, mix melted baking chocolate with corn syrup. Add vanilla, butter, powdered sugar and milk. Whisk thoroughly until smooth. Spread over top layer of Graham crackers.
4. Cover and refrigerate cake for 2 hours or overnight.

Chocolate Peanut Butter Pie

SERVINGS: 12
PREP TIME: 15 min.
TOTAL TIME: 20 min. + refrigeration

Ingredients

- 1.5 cups graham cracker crumbs
- 2 tablespoons sugar
- 6 tablespoons (3 oz.) unsalted butter, melted

Chocolate Crunch Layer:

- 4 oz. milk chocolate
- 2.5 oz.(½ cup) honey roasted peanuts, rough chopped

Peanut Butter Filling:

- 13.5 oz.(1.5 cups) peanut butter
- 12 oz. cream cheese
- 1.5 cups heavy cream
- 1.5 cups powdered sugar
- 2 teaspoons vanilla extract

Garnish:

- Dark chocolate glaze or sauce for drizzle
- Additional ¼ cup honey roasted peanuts, rough chopped

Instructions

1. Mix graham cracker crumbs, sugar and melted butter together. Press into 9" pie pan. Chill until firm, about an hour.
2. Melt milk chocolate in microwave in 30 second increments until melted.
3. Spread evenly on chilled graham cracker crust.
4. Sprinkle chopped peanuts on top of chocolate and refrigerate until hardened.
5. Mix peanut butter and cream cheese till smooth slowly adding in 1 cup of the powdered sugar. Add vanilla extract and continue to mix until everything is combined.

6. In separate bowl, whip heavy cream with remaining half cup powdered sugar until stiff.
7. Fold whipped cream into peanut butter mix and pour into pie plate, smoothing the top with a spatula. Refrigerate.
8. Drizzle melted dark chocolate, chocolate sauce, or chocolate glaze over the top of the well chilled pie.

Fresh Strawberry Pie

SERVINGS: 8
PREP/TOTAL TIME: 1 hour

Ingredients

- 25 chocolate wafers
- 3 oz. bittersweet chocolate, finely chopped
- 2 teaspoons canola oil
- Cooking spray
- 6 oz. ⅓-less-fat cream cheese, softened
- ⅓ cup powdered sugar
- ¾ teaspoon vanilla extract
- 2 cups frozen fat-free whipped topping, thawed
- 2 tablespoons seedless strawberry fruit spread
- 1 tablespoon Chambord (raspberry-flavored liqueur)
- ½ teaspoon fresh lemon juice
- 1 pound small strawberries, hulled and cut in half

Instructions

1. Place chocolate wafers in a food processor, and process until finely ground. Place the chopped chocolate in a small microwave-safe bowl. Microwave at HIGH for 45 seconds or until chocolate melts, stirring every 15 seconds. Add melted chocolate and oil to a blender or processor and process until well combined. Gently press the mix into bottom and up sides of a 9-inch pie plate or removable-bottom tart pan coated with cooking spray. Place in freezer 15 minutes or until set.
2. Place cream cheese, sugar, and vanilla in a medium bowl. Beat with a mixer at medium speed until smooth. Fold in whipped topping. Carefully spread over bottom of crust. Place fruit spread in a large microwave-safe bowl and microwave at HIGH 10 seconds or until softened. Add Chambord and juice. Stir with a whisk until smooth. Add berry halves and toss to combine. Arrange berry halves over pie.
3. Chill for 30 minutes before serving.

Strawberry Angel Cake

SERVINGS: 16
PREP TIME: 10 min.
TOTAL TIME: 1 hour + refrigeration

Ingredients

- 4 cups sliced strawberries
- ¾ cup sugar, divided
- 2 tablespoons evaporated skim milk
- 1 (8-oz.) block ⅓-less-fat cream cheese, softened
- 1 (10-inch) round angel food cake
- 3 tablespoons triple sec (orange-flavored liqueur) or orange juice, divided
- 1 (8-oz.) tub frozen reduced-calorie whipped topping, thawed
- 2 tablespoons sliced almonds, toasted

Instructions

1. Combine strawberries and ¼ cup sugar in a small bowl. Cover and let stand 1 hour. In a medium bowl, combine ½ cup sugar, milk, and cream cheese. Beat at medium speed of a mixer until smooth.
2. Cut cake horizontally into 3 layers. Place bottom layer, cut side up, on a serving plate. Brush with 1 tablespoon liqueur, and spread half of cream cheese mixture over cake.
3. Spoon one-third of strawberries over cream cheese mixture using a slotted spoon.
4. Repeat layers, ending with cake and liqueur. Spread whipped topping over top and sides of cake.
5. Cover and chill 30 minutes.
6. Arrange remaining strawberries on top of cake before serving. Sprinkle with almonds.

Cheesecake Mini-Desserts

Ingredients

- 8 oz. package of cream cheese, softened
- 2 tablespoons lemon juice
- 1 teaspoon vanilla
- 14 oz. can, sweetened condensed milk (not evaporated milk)
- small baked shells (croustades)
- desired fruit (strawberries, blueberries, raspberries, blackberries, kiwi)

Instructions

1. In a small mixing bowl, beat cream cheese and lemon juice until smooth.
2. Add vanilla and sweetened condensed milk to the cream cheese mix, beating 45 to 60 seconds until smooth.
3. Spoon this filling mixture into small baked pastry shells, approximately 1 tablespoon or less per shell.
4. Garnish with fresh berries such as blueberries, raspberries, or blackberries. Some larger fruits, such as strawberries or kiwi, can be sliced into smaller pieces.
5. Refrigerate 1 hour or until mixture thickens.

White Chocolate Cake Batter Fudge

SERVINGS: 8
PREP TIME: 10 min.
TOTAL TIME: 30 min.

Ingredients

- 1 (14 oz.) can sweetened condensed milk
- 3 ½ cups white chocolate chips (about 1¾ bags)
- 3 teaspoons vanilla extract
- ½ teaspoons almond extract

Instructions

1. Pour milk and white chocolate into a microwave-safe bowl. Microwave for 2-3 minutes, or until white chocolate is almost completely melted. Avoid overheating. Stir until completely blended, melted, and smooth.
2. Add vanilla and almond extract and thoroughly combine. Add a handful of rainbow sprinkles and quickly fold in because they will melt.
3. Transfer to an aluminum-foil lined or well-greased 8×8 inch baking pan for very thick fudge, or an 11x7 inch pan for thinner fudge. Set at room temperature or in the refrigerator.
4. Once set, cut into cubes.

Nutella Cake

SERVINGS: 4
PREP/TOTAL TIME: 15 min.

Ingredients

- 1 cup refined flour
- 1/2 cup powdered sugar
- 1 tablespoon baking powder
- 1/2 cup refined oil
- 1/2 cup Nutella
- 1 egg

Instructions

1. Sieve baking powder, flour and sugar in a microwaveable bowl.
2. Whisk an egg in a separate bowl and add oil and Nutella. Whisk until well mixed.
3. Add egg mixture to the dry ingredient bowl and mix well. Add 2-3 tablespoon of cold milk if mixture is too thick.
4. Place the microwaveable bowl in the microwave and cook for 2-3 minutes.
5. It is done when a toothpick inserted comes out clean.

Mississippi Mud Ice Cream Pie

SERVINGS: 12-15
PREP TIME: 10 min.
TOTAL TIME: 40 min. + refrigeration

Ingredients

- 1 (15 oz.) package of Oreo's
- ½ cup butter, melted
- 1 (12 oz.) container fudge ice cream topping
- ½ gallon vanilla ice cream
- 2 cups nuts, chopped (optional)
- Whipped topping
- Crushed Oreos, to sprinkle on top

Instructions

1. Crush the package of Oreo's in blender, or in a Ziploc bag with a rolling pin, and mix with melted butter. Press cookie crust into 9x13 inch cake pan or 2 pie pans.
2. Soften ice cream at room temperature for about 30-35 minutes. Spread ice cream onto the Oreo crust and freeze for 2 hours.
3. Pour warm fudge topping over ice cream. Freeze until well chilled (around 6-8 hours).
4. Cut into serving-size pieces. Top pieces with whipped topping, nuts, drizzled hot fudge, and crushed Oreos.

Peanut Butter Cream Cheese Pie

SERVINGS: 5
PREP/TOTAL TIME: 10 minutes + refrigeration

Ingredients

- 1 chocolate graham cracker or cookie pie crust (homemade or store-bought)
- 8 oz. cream cheese
- 1 cup peanut butter
- ½ cup granulated sugar
- 1 teaspoon pure vanilla extract
- 8 oz. frozen whipped topping, thawed
- whipped cream, chocolate syrup, and grated chocolate (garnish)

Instructions

1. Beat cream cheese and sugar until smooth. Blend in peanut butter and vanilla. Fold in whipped topping. Spoon mixture into prepared pie crust. Refrigerate for at least 4 hours.
2. Garnish with whipped cream and chocolate syrup, with a sprinkling of grated chocolate.

Peanut Butter Eclair Cake

Ingredients

- 18 chocolate graham crackers
- 1 box (3.5oz) vanilla instant pudding mix
- 1 cup milk
- ½ cup creamy peanut butter
- 8 oz. Cool Whip
- 16 Reese's Peanut butter cups

Frosting:
- 2 oz. unsweetened chocolate
- 3 tablespoons unsalted butter
- 1 tablespoon corn syrup
- 1½ cup powdered sugar
- 3 tablespoons milk

Instructions

1. In a large mixing bowl, beat vanilla pudding mix with milk, until there are no lumps. Beat in peanut butter until smooth. Fold in the Cool Whip, set aside.
2. In a 9inch square baking dish, layer 6 grahams. Top with half of the pudding mix. Top with 6 more crackers and the 16 Reese's PB cups. Top with the remaining of the pudding mix. Finish by topping with the remaining 6 graham crackers.
3. For the frosting, heat unsweetened chocolate with butter and corn syrup on medium heat in a small saucepan. Whisk until smooth. Remove from heat and whisk in the powdered sugar and milk. Frost the top of the graham cracker layer and place in refrigerator.
4. Refrigerate for 4 hours or overnight. Cut and enjoy!

Golden Oreo No Melt Ice Cream Pie

SERVINGS: 16
PREP TIME: 20 min.
TOTAL TIME: 3 hours

Ingredients

- 16 Golden Oreos, chopped
- 4 squares white chocolate
- 8 oz. cream cheese, softened
- ¼ cup sugar
- 1 container (8 oz.) Cool Whip, thawed

Instructions

1. Spread chopped Oreos onto a pie plate.
2. Microwave white chocolate in a medium bowl for 1 minute. Stir to completely melt chocolate. Set aside.
3. In different bowl, beat cream cheese and sugar until light and fluffy. Stir in Cool Whip. Place 1½ cup Cool Whip Mixture in the bowl with melted white chocolate. Gently stir.
4. Spread white chocolate mixture over the chopped Oreos. Spread the remaining Cool Whip mixture over the white chocolate mixture in the pan. Press rest of the chopped Oreos into this layer.
5. Cover and freeze for 3 hours or until firm.

Grasshopper Pie

SERVINGS: 10-12
PREP/TOTAL TIME: 20 min. + freezing

Ingredients

- Deep Dish pie pan (9 or 10" diameter, 2" deep)
- 2¼ cups chocolate wafer crumbs
- 6 tablespoons of unsalted butter, melted
- 38 large marshmallows
- 1 cup Half and Half
- ½ cup green Crème de Menthe liqueur
- 1 ⅓ cups heavy whipping cream

Instructions

1. Butter the pie pan. In a large bowl, combine the chocolate wafer crumbs and melted butter. (Reserve 2 tablespoons of the crumbs for later use). Stir until combined. Pour crumb mixture into pie pan. Using back of a large spoon and press crumbs into the pie pan evenly on the bottom and sides to form a crust. Place in the freezer.
2. Combine marshmallows and half and half in the top of a double broiler or in a metal heat proof bowl placed over a sauce pan of boiling water. Cook, constantly stirring until marshmallows have melted completely. Remove from heat.
3. Add Crème de Menthe into the marshmallow mix and stir or whisk to fully combine. Allow the mixture to slightly cool, about 10 minutes.
4. Using a standing or hand held mixer, whip heavy whipping cream until firm peaks appear. Stir into the green marshmallow mixture. Whisk lightly at the end to ensure the mixture is combined well.
5. Pour into prepared pie crust. Sprinkle the remaining 2 tablespoons of the crumbs on the top and place in the freezer. Freeze until firm.

Strawberry Icebox Cake

SERVINGS: 5
PREP/TOTAL TIME: 20 min. + refrigeration

Ingredients

- 2 pounds fresh strawberries, washed
- 3½ cups whipping cream, divided
- ⅓ cup confectioners' sugar
- 1 teaspoon vanilla
- ½ teaspoon almond extract (optional)
- 4 sleeves (about 19 oz., or 24 to 28 whole crackers) graham crackers
- 2 oz. dark chocolate, finely chopped

Instructions

1. Set aside a few of the best looking strawberries for the garnish. Hull the remainder of the strawberries and slice each into thin slices.
2. Whip 3 cups of cream until it holds stiff peaks.
3. Add confectioners' sugar, vanilla, and almond extract (if using) and whip until well- combined.
4. Spread a small spoonful of whipped cream on the bottom of a 9×13 inch baking pan. Lay down six graham crackers. Lightly cover top of the graham crackers with a thin layer of whipped cream, and then a single layer of strawberries. Repeat three more times, until you have four layers of graham crackers. Spread the last of the whipped cream over the top and lightly swirl with a spoon. Add a few more strawberries.
5. To make the ganache, heat remaining cream until bubbles form around the edges, and pour over the chopped chocolate. Let it stand for a few minutes, then whisk until the mixture is thick and glossy. Drizzle this over the layered dessert with a spoon, or transfer to a squeeze bottle to drizzle.
6. Refrigerate for at least four hours, or until the crackers have softened.
7. Garnish with additional berries and serve.

Fluffy Blueberry Cheesecake

SERVINGS: 5-7
PREP TIME: 5 min.
TOTAL TIME: 1 hour

Ingredients

- 1 (8 oz.) package cream cheese, softened
- ⅓ cup sugar
- 1 (8 oz.) container Cool Whip, thawed
- 1 prepared graham cracker crust
- 21 oz. can blueberry (or cherry) pie filling

Instructions

1. In a large bowl, beat cream cheese and sugar on medium speed until smooth and the sugar has dissolved. Gently stir in whipped topping.
2. Spoon into pie crust and spread to the edge of crust.
3. Refrigerate for at least 1 hour.
4. Top with pie filling just before serving.

Key Lime Chocolate Squares

SERVINGS: 16
PREP TIME: 15 min.
TOTAL TIME: 1 hour

Ingredients

- ½ cup butter
- 1 (12 oz.) bag chocolate chips, divided
- 2 cups chocolate wafers pulsed into crumbs
- ¼ cup butter softened
- 3 tablespoon key lime juice
- ½ teaspoon vanilla
- 2 tablespoon milk
- 2 cups powdered sugar
- ⅓ cup butter

Instructions

1. Grease an 8x8 pan. In a small saucepan, melt ½ cup butter and ¼ cup chocolate chips, constantly stirring. Remove from heat once butter has melted. Add chocolate wafer crumbs and stir until well mixed. Press into bottom of the pan. Set in fridge for 10-20 minutes.
2. In a bowl, beat ¼ cup softened butter, the key lime juice, extract and milk. Slowly add in powdered sugar on low until smooth. Spread over crumb layer. Set in fridge for another 10-20 minutes.
3. Melt remaining chocolate and butter on low. Stir constantly until smooth. Pour over key lime layer. Keep in refrigerator until set, about 15-30 minutes.

Apple Pie Cheesecakes

SERVINGS: 10
PREP TIME: 15 min.
TOTAL TIME: 20 min. + refrigeration

Ingredients

- 1 tablespoon unsalted butter
- ¾ cup apples, peeled and diced
- 1 teaspoon cinnamon
- ½ teaspoons allspice
- ¼ teaspoons ground nutmeg
- 1 pkg. (8 oz.) cream cheese, softened
- 1 can (14 oz.) sweetened condensed milk
- 1 teaspoon lemon juice concentrate
- 6 oz. Cool Whip
- ½ pkg. refrigerated pie crust dough (unrolled)
- 2 tablespoons butter
- 2 tablespoons cinnamon/sugar mixture
- ¼ cup toffee bits (Heath)

Instructions

1. In a small non-stick skillet, melt 1 tablespoon butter over medium heat. Add apples, cinnamon, allspice and nutmeg. Stir over medium heat for about 3-4 minutes, until apples have softened slightly. Set aside to cool.
2. In a mixer, beat cream cheese with condensed milk and lemon juice for 5 minutes. Add in cooled apple mixture. Fold in Cool Whip. Sprinkle with toffee bits.
3. Refrigerate 3 hours until ready to serve.
4. Melt 2 tablespoons of butter. Spread over unrolled pie crust and sprinkle with cinnamon sugar mix. Use a small apple cookie cutter and place cut outs on a parchment paper lined baking sheet.

Peanut Butter Pie

SERVINGS: 20
PREP/TOTA TIME: 25 min. + refrigeration

Ingredients

- 1 cup powdered sugar
- 1 cup natural-style, reduced-fat creamy peanut butter
- 1 (8-oz.) block ⅓-less-fat cream cheese, softened
- 1 (14-oz.) can fat-free sweetened condensed milk
- 12 oz. frozen fat-free whipped topping, thawed
- 2 (6-oz.) reduced-fat graham cracker crusts
- 20 teaspoons fat-free chocolate sundae syrup

Instructions

1. Combine powdered sugar, peanut butter, and cream cheese in a large bowl. Beat with a mixer at medium speed until smooth. Add milk and beat until combined. Fold in whipped topping. Divide mixture evenly between crusts.
2. Chill 8 hours or until set. Cut into wedges and drizzle with chocolate syrup.

Banana Split Icebox Cake

SERVINGS: 10
PREP TIME: 15 min.
TOTAL TIME: 35 min. + refrigeration

Ingredients

- 1 carton (16 oz.) frozen whipped topping, thawed
- 1 cup (8 oz.) sour cream
- 1 package (3.4 oz.) instant vanilla pudding mix
- 1 can (8 oz.) crushed pineapple, drained
- 24 whole graham crackers
- 2 medium bananas, sliced thin
- Toppings: additional sliced bananas and sliced fresh strawberries

Chocolate Drizzle:

- ¼ cup heavy cream
- ¼ cup semi-sweet chocolate chips

Instructions

1. In a large bowl, mix the whipped topping, sour cream, and pudding mix until well mixed. Fold in pineapple.
2. Fill a Ziploc bag with pudding mix and cut off corner of the bag.
3. On a flat serving plate arrange four graham crackers in a rectangle. Pipe about 1 cup of the pudding mixture over the crackers and top with ¼ cup banana slices. Repeat layers five times. Cover and refrigerate for at least 8 hours or overnight. Graham crackers should be soft.
4. Make chocolate drizzle. Heat cream in the microwave until hot (about 20-30 seconds). Place chocolate chips in a small bowl and pour hot cream over the chips. Let sit for a moment and stir until chocolate is smooth. Let cool slightly while preparing bananas and strawberries for the topping.

Nutella Cake

Ingredients

- 1 cup refined flour
- 1/2 cup powdered sugar
- 1 tablespoon baking powder
- 1/2 cup refined oil
- 1/2 cup Nutella
- 1 egg

Instructions

1. Sieve baking powder, flour and sugar in a microwaveable bowl.
2. Whisk an egg in a separate bowl and add oil and Nutella. Whisk until well mixed.
3. Add egg mixture to the dry ingredient bowl and mix well. Add 2-3 tablespoon of cold milk if mixture is too thick.
4. Place the microwaveable bowl in the microwave and cook for 2-3 minutes.
5. It is done when a toothpick inserted comes out clean.

FRUIT DESSERTS

Strawberry Mousse

SERVINGS: 2-4
PREP TIME: 25 min.
TOTAL TIME: 30 min. + refrigeration

Ingredients

- 1 cup finely chopped strawberries
- ½ cup sugar, divided
- 5 tablespoons water, divided
- ¾ teaspoon unflavored gelatin
- Dash of salt
- 2 large egg whites
- ¼ teaspoon vanilla extract
- ½ cup heavy whipping cream

Instructions

1. Combine chopped strawberries and 1 tablespoon sugar in the bowl of a food processor, and toss gently. Let stand for 10 minutes. Process until smooth.
2. In a large bowl, pour 2 tablespoons water and sprinkle with gelatin. Let stand for 5 minutes.
3. Place 6 tablespoons sugar, remaining 3 tablespoons water, and dash of salt in a small heavy saucepan over medium-high heat. Bring to a boil, stirring until sugar dissolves. Cook, without stirring for about 4 more minutes. Add egg whites to gelatin mixture and beat with a mixer at high speed until foamy. Gradually add remaining 1 tablespoon sugar, beating at high speed until soft peaks form. Pour hot sugar syrup into egg white mixture, beating at medium speed and then at high speed until stiff peaks form. Beat in vanilla.
4. Place cream in a large bowl and beat with a mixer at high speed until stiff peaks form. Gently fold one-fourth of egg white mix into whipped cream. Fold in the remaining egg white mix and then fold in strawberry mixture. Spoon about ½ cup mousse into 6 dessert glasses.
5. Chill 2 hours or until set.

Tropical Sherbet

Ingredients

- 1 (12-oz.) package frozen mango chunks (about 2 ½ cups)
- 1 cup frozen pineapple chunks
- 1 (6-oz.) carton lemon low-fat yogurt
- 1 teaspoon grated lime rind

Instructions

1. Remove mango and pineapple from freezer. Let stand at room temperature for 10 minutes.
2. Combine mango, pineapple, yogurt, and rind in a food processor. Process until smooth.
3. Serve immediately (for soft texture) or freeze in an airtight container for 2 hours (for firmer texture).

Blueberry-Orange Parfaits

SERVINGS: 4
PREP/TOTAL TIME: 15 min.

Ingredients

- 1 ½ tablespoons Demerara or turbinado sugar
- ½ teaspoon grated orange rind
- 2 (7-oz.) containers reduced-fat plain Greek-style yogurt
- 2 cups fresh blueberries
- 2 cups orange sections (about 2 large)
- ¼ cup wheat germ

Instructions

1. Combine first 3 ingredients in a small bowl, stirring until blended.
2. Spoon ¼ cup blueberries into 4 tall glasses. Spoon about 2 ½ tablespoons yogurt mixture over blueberries in each glass. Add ¼ cup orange to each serving.
3. Repeat layers with remaining blueberries, yogurt mix, and orange.
4. Sprinkle 1 tablespoon wheat germ over each serving and serve immediately.

Banana Split Oreo Dessert

SERVINGS: 24 slices
PREP/TOTAL TIME: 20 min. + refrigeration

Ingredients

- 2 ¼ cups crushed Oreo cookie crumbs, divided
- ⅓ cup butter, melted
- 2 - 8 oz. packages cream cheese, softened
- ½ cup sugar
- 2 mashed ripe bananas
- 5 cups Cool Whip, divided
- 3 sliced ripe bananas
- 2½ cups sliced fresh strawberries
- 2 - 3.9 oz. boxes instant chocolate pudding
- 2 cups milk
- Oreo cookies, broken in half

Instructions

1. Combine 2 cups Oreo crumbs and butter and press into bottom of a 9x13 inch pan. Refrigerate.
2. Beat cream cheese and sugar until creamy. Add mashed bananas and beat again. Slowly mix in 2 cups Cool Whip. Spread out and spoon onto the crust.
3. Place sliced bananas over the banana cheesecake layer. Top with strawberry slices.
4. Whisk the pudding mixes and milk together. Fold in 1 cup of Cool Whip. Spoon gently over strawberry layer and spread out. Top with the remaining 2 cups of Cool Whip and spread. Refrigerate for a few hours.
5. Sprinkle with remaining ¼ crumbs. Cut into 24 squares and top each with an Oreo half.

Peach and Raspberry Pavlova Parfaits

Ingredients

- ½ cup (4 oz.) ⅓-less-fat cream cheese
- ¼ cup sugar, divided
- 1 cup vanilla fat-free yogurt
- 2 cups sliced peeled peaches (about 6 to 7 peaches)
- 1 cup raspberries
- 1 cup vanilla meringue cookie crumbs, coarsely crushed
- 12 vanilla meringue mini cookies

Instructions

1. Place cream cheese and 3 tablespoons sugar in a medium bowl. Beat with a mixer at high speed for 2 minutes or until smooth. Beat in yogurt until blended.
2. Combine 1 tablespoon sugar, peaches, and raspberries in a large bowl. Toss to coat and let stand 5 minutes.
3. Spoon 2 tablespoons cheese mixture into 6 (8-oz.) glasses. Top each with ¼ cup peach mixture and 2 ½ tablespoons cookie crumbs. Repeat layers once with remaining cheese mixture and remaining peach mixture. Top each with 2 whole cookies.
4. Cover and chill until ready to serve.

Strawberries with Orange-Ricotta Cream

SERVINGS: 2
PREP/TOTAL TIME: 10 min. + refrigeration

Ingredients

- ½ cup part-skim ricotta cheese
- ½ cup vanilla low-fat yogurt
- 1 tablespoon sugar
- ½ teaspoon grated orange rind
- ½ teaspoon vanilla extract
- 1 cup quartered strawberries
- 2 whole strawberries (optional)

Instructions

1. Combine the first 5 ingredients in a blender and process until smooth.
2. Spoon cheese mixture into a small bowl. Cover and chill for 3 hours.
3. Spoon ½ cup quartered strawberries into each of 2 small bowls. Top each with 2 tablespoons cheese mixture.
4. Garnish each serving with a whole strawberry, if desired.

Frozen Key Lime Margarita Squares

SERVINGS: 16
PREP/TOTAL TIME: 15 min. + freezing

Ingredients

Crust:

- 2 cups graham cracker crumbs
- 2 tablespoons sugar
- 3 tablespoons butter, melted

Filling:

- 16 oz. cream cheese, softened
- ½ cup sugar
- ½ cup key lime juice
- 1 lime zested
- 2 tablespoons tequila
- Whipped cream

Instructions

1. Line an 8x8 inch baking pan with foil.
2. Combine graham cracker crumbs, sugar, and melted butter. Press into the bottom or the baking pan. Place in freezer.
3. In the bowl of a mixer, add cream cheese, sugar, key lime juice, lime zest and tequila. Beat on low until it starts to come together. Beat on medium-high for 5 minutes, until it is smooth and fluffy.
4. Pour filling over the prepared crust and freeze overnight.

Limoncello Freeze

Ingredients

- ¼ cup lemon curd
- 2 ½ tablespoons Limoncello (lemon-flavored liqueur)
- 2 cups vanilla low-fat ice cream
- 4 vanilla meringue cookies, crushed (about ½ cup)

Instructions

1. Combine curd and liqueur in a small bowl. Stir with a whisk to blend.
2. Add ice cream to curd mixture and stir to blend.
3. Spoon ½ cup ice cream mixture into 4 bowls. Top each with 1 crushed meringue cookie.

Strawberries in Lemon Syrup

SERVINGS: 4
PREP/TOTAL TIME: 25 min.

Ingredients

- 4 cups quartered small strawberries
- ¼ cup fresh lemon juice
- ¼ cup sugar
- ¼ cup whipping cream

Instructions

1. Place berries, juice, and sugar in a large bowl. Toss gently to coat. Cover and chill 20 minutes.
2. Place cream in a medium bowl. Stir constantly with a whisk until soft peaks form.
3. Serve whipped cream with berry mixture.

Banana Cream Pie Smoothie

SERVINGS: 2
PREP/TOTAL TIME: 10 min. + refrigeration

Ingredients

- 1 cup sliced ripe banana (about 1 large)
- 1 cup vanilla low-fat yogurt
- ½ cup 1% low-fat milk
- 2 tablespoons whole wheat graham cracker crumbs (about ½ cookie sheet)
- 1 tablespoon nonfat dry milk
- ½ teaspoon vanilla extract
- 3 ice cubes (about ¼ cup)
- Graham cracker crumbs

Instructions

1. Arrange banana slices in a single layer on a baking sheet, and freeze until firm (about 1 hour).
2. Place frozen banana and remaining ingredients in a blender. Process until smooth.
3. Sprinkle with graham cracker crumbs. Serve immediately.

Cherry Limeade Fruit Dip

SERVINGS: 10
PREP TIME: 10 min.
TOTAL TIME: 30 min.

Ingredients

- 8 oz. cream cheese, softened
- 6 oz. lime yogurt
- ½ cup powdered sugar
- 2 tablespoons protein powder
- Juice of 1 lime (approx. 2 tablespoons)
- 1 teaspoon lime zest, optional
- 8 oz. Cool Whip
- 3 tablespoons cherry jam/preserves or crushed fresh cherries

Instructions

1. Combine cream cheese, yogurt, powdered sugar, and protein powder in the bowl of a mixer or blender.
2. Slowly add lime juice, zest, and Cool Whip until well-mixed.
3. In a small bowl, swirl cherry preserves along the inside walls of the bowl and add limeade dip.
4. Chill for at least 30 minutes.

Passionfruit Blueberry Cheesecake Parfait

SERVINGS: 6
PREP/TOTAL TIME: 30 min.

Ingredients

Passionfruit Curd
- 2 eggs
- 3 egg yolks
- 1 cup sugar
- 3 tablespoons (0.75 oz.) cornstarch
- 1 cup passionfruit puree
- 4 oz. unsalted butter, at room temperature

Cheesecake Parfait
- 1½ cups graham cracker crumbs
- 4 tablespoons unsalted butter, melted
- ½ teaspoon lemon zest
- 1½ cup heavy cream
- 4 oz. cream cheese, room temperature
- ¼ cup sugar
- splash of pure vanilla extract
- 1 pint blueberries

Instructions

1. Whisk egg, egg yolks and sugar together in a medium sauce pan until smooth. Whisk corn starch with a bit of passionfruit puree. Whisk the rest of the passionfruit puree and passionfruit mix into the egg mixture. Continue to whisk over medium heat until thick, around 10-15 minutes. Keep the bottom from burning.
2. Over low-heat, slowly whisk in the pieces of butter
3. Move curd to a bowl and allow to chill and thicken in the refrigerator. Line the top of the curd with plastic wrap to prevent skin from forming.
4. In a small bowl, combine graham cracker crumbs, melted butter and lemon zest. Set aside.

5. In a stand mixer with the whisk attachment, combine heavy cream and cream cheese until well mixed. Add sugar and vanilla and turn the speed to high and allow the mixture to reach a stiff peak
6. Layer the three ingredients in a decorative dish: Start with the cream cheese filling, then by the curd, the crumbs and the blueberries. Top with a small amount of cream cheese filling and blueberries.

OTHER TREATS

Rice Krispie Fluffernutter Treats

SERVINGS: 32 squares
PREP/TOTAL TIME: 1 hour

Ingredients

- 10 oz. bag regular sized marshmallows
- ¼ cup unsalted butter
- ½ cup creamy peanut butter
- 5 cup Rice Krispies cereal
- 1¼ cup mini marshmallows
- 1 bag (10 oz.) Reese's peanut butter morsels, melted
- 2 bags (8 oz. each) Reese's mini Peanut Butter Cups

Instructions

1. Melt butter over medium heat in a large pot. Add marshmallows and turn heat to low. Stir until smooth. Remove from heat and quickly stir in peanut butter. Add cereal.
2. Fold in mini marshmallows. Pour Krispies treats into a 9 inch square baking dish lined with parchment paper or buttered foil. Do not press them in tightly. Spread melted peanut butter morsels over top.
3. Top melted peanut butter morsels with the peanut butter cups. Press them in so they stick.
4. Allow to set, about one hour. Cut into squares and store in an airtight container.

Bacon Nutella Krispies

SERVINGS: 20-24 bars
PREP TIME: 10 min.
TOTAL TIME: 20 min.

Ingredients

- 4 tablespoons butter
- 1 10 oz. pkg. regular size marshmallows
- 1 teaspoon kosher salt
- ½ cup Nutella or any chocolate hazelnut spread
- ½ pkg. pepper bacon, crispy and diced
- 6 cups Rice Krispies cereal

Instructions

1. Spray 13x9-inch pan with cooking spray and set aside.
2. In a large saucepan over low heat, melt butter until slightly browned, careful not to burn the butter.
3. Add marshmallows and kosher salt. Stir until marshmallows have melted.
4. Remove from heat and stir in Nutella until melted.
5. Add cereal and crispy bacon. Stir until well-combined.
6. Pour cereal mix into the pan and press firmly with a sheet of wax paper placed on top.
7. Cool and cut into 2-inch squares or cookie-cutter shapes.

Key Lime Melt-Aways

SERVINGS: 12
PREP/TOTAL TIME: 15 min. + refrigeration

Ingredients

- 1½ cup prepared sugar cookies, crumbled
- ⅔ cup unsalted butter, softened
- 1½ cup powdered sugar
- 3 tablespoons key lime juice
- 2 key limes, zest
- 3-4 key limes, sliced, for garnish

Instructions

1. In a medium bowl, combine cookie crumbs and ⅓ cup butter. Press into bottom of a 9-inch square pan. Refrigerate until firm.
2. In a small bowl, combine powdered sugar, ⅓ cup butter, key lime juice, and key lime zest. Beat at medium-high speed until light and smooth. Spread over crust.
3. Cut bars into 1½ inch squares and top each with a key lime slice.
4. Cover bars and refrigerate until firm, about 2 hours. Remove lime slice before serving.

S'mores Krispie Treats

SERVINGS: 16
PREP TIME: 15 min.
TOTAL TIME: 45 min.

Ingredients

- 2 (16 oz.) bags mini marshmallows, divided
- 1½ sticks (12 tablespoons) salted butter
- pinch salt
- 1.5 (12 oz.) boxes of Golden Grahams cereal
- 1 (12 oz.) bag semi-sweet chocolate chips

Instructions

1. Melt butter in a medium bowl. Add all but 1 cup of the mini marshmallows and salt. Stir over low heat until marshmallows are melted. Reserve remaining marshmallows.
2. In a large bowl, toss Golden Grahams cereal with the marshmallow mix until cereal is coated. Add all but ½ cup of the chocolate chips and mix until the chips are evenly distributed throughout.
3. Grease and line a 13x9x2 inch pan with parchment paper. Press marshmallow mix into the pan, making it even and flat. Sprinkle reserved chocolate chips over the mix, and reserved marshmallows over the chocolate chips.
4. Chill thoroughly before cutting squares, and serve at room temperature.

White Trash

SERVINGS: 12
PREP TIME: 15 min.
TOTAL TIME: 20 min.

Ingredients

- 1 cup Honey Nut Cheerios
- ½ cup Cocoa Puffs
- 1 cup Fruit Loops
- 1 cup M&M's and Hershey eggs
- 1 cup broken pretzel sticks
- 12 oz. Vanilla CandiQuik (almond bark, vanilla bark)

Instructions

1. Melt vanilla CandiQuik according to package directions. Mix in dry ingredients.
2. Pour on wax paper and let cool. Break into pieces and refrigerate or serve.

Samoa's Rice Krispie Treats

Ingredients

- 4 tablespoons butter
- 10 oz. mini marshmallows
- 5 cups crisp rice cereal
- 1 cup + 2 cups coconut
- 1 batch caramel sauce
- 1 bag (10-12 oz.) chocolate chips

Instructions

1. Melt butter in a saucepan, careful not to burn it. Add marshmallows and stir until completely melted. Pour marshmallow mix into a bowl with cereal and 1 cup of coconut. Set aside.
2. Mix 2 cups coconut with caramel sauce. Set aside.
3. Melt chocolate chips in a microwave safe bowl. In 30 second intervals in the microwave, stir between each.
4. Pour ¾ of the chocolate into the bottom of a 9x13 inch pan. Press half the Krispie treat mix over the chocolate. Pour caramel coconut mixture evenly over the top. Top and press with remaining Krispie treat mixture. Drizzle remaining chocolate over the top.
5. Place the pan in the refrigerator and chill for 30-60 minutes, until set. Cut into 12 large or 20 small bars.

Brown Butter Churro Crispy Treats

SERVINGS: 16
PREP TIME: 15 min.
TOTAL TIME: 30 min.

Ingredients

- 6 tablespoons unsalted butter
- 1 tablespoon dark brown sugar
- 1 tablespoon cinnamon
- ½ teaspoon pure vanilla extract
- 10 oz. miniature marshmallows
- ¼ teaspoon kosher salt
- 6 cups cinnamon rice squares (Cinnamon Chex)

Instructions

1. Butter or coat an 8-inch square pan with non-stick spray.
2. Melt butter over medium-low heat in a large pot. Continue to heat until butter melts and starts to turn brown and smell nutty. Stir frequently, scraping up bits from bottom and ensure butter does not burn. Turn off heat, and stir in brown sugar, cinnamon and vanilla.
3. Add marshmallows and stir to melt. Turn heat on low and stir until marshmallows are smooth and no white streaks remain.
4. Remove pot and stir in the cereal and salt. Spread it quickly into prepared pan. Lightly coat a sheet of wax paper and evenly press it into pan corners.
5. Let cool 15 minutes, cut bars and serve.

Cookie Dough S'mores

SERVINGS: 10
PREP/TOTAL TIME: 25 min.

Ingredients

- ½ cup butter, softened
- ¾ cup brown sugar
- 1 teaspoon vanilla
- 1 cup flour
- pinch salt
- ¾ cup miniature chocolate chips
- 5 large flat puffed marshmallows
- 20 graham cracker squares
- 1 package (16 oz.) chocolate CandiQuik
- sprinkles

Instructions

1. Combine the butter, sugar, and vanilla. Add flour and salt, and mix well. Stir in chips and set aside.
2. Cut the marshmallows in half. Place cut side down on a graham cracker square. Take a ball of dough and mold it into the shape and size of marshmallow. Place on top of the marshmallow and top with another graham cracker square. Lightly press down.
3. Place the unwrapped tray of CandiQuik in the microwave. Heat for 1 minute. Stir and heat again for 20-30 seconds. Stir until melted and creamy.
4. Using a fork, place s'mores one at a time in melted chocolate. Spread the chocolate over the crackers with a spoon. Gently remove with a fork. Hold over chocolate tray and tap wrist holding the chocolate. When the excess chocolate has dripped off, place on wax paper and top with sprinkles. Let set.
5. Store in a loosely sealed container.

Reese's Peanut Butter Cookie Dough Dip

SERVINGS: 10-12
PREP TIME: 5 min.
TOTAL TIME: 15 min.

Ingredients

- ½ cup unsalted butter
- ½ cup light brown sugar
- ¼ cup creamy peanut butte
- 8 oz. cream cheese, softened
- 1¾ cup powdered sugar
- 1 teaspoon vanilla extract
- ½ cup semi-sweet mini chocolate chips
- 8 oz. pkg. Reese's peanut butter cup minis (or 1½ cup chopped Reese's cups)

Instructions

1. Melt butter in a small saucepan over medium heat. Whisk in sugar and heat until sugar dissolves (around 1 minute). Remove from heat and immediately add vanilla. Allow to cool to room temperature.
2. In a large mixing bowl, beat the cream cheese, powdered sugar and peanut butter until creamy (about 3-4 minutes). On low speed, add in the cooled brown sugar mixture. Mix until well combined.
3. Fold in mini chocolate chips and mini Reese's cups.
4. Serve immediately or store in refrigerator until ready to serve.
5. Enjoy with pretzels, animal crackers, or graham sticks.

Oven Peanut Brittle

SERVINGS: 16
PREP TIME: 10 min.
TOTAL TIME: 30 min.

Ingredients

- 1½ cups dry roasted peanuts
- 1 cup white sugar
- 1/2 cup light corn syrup
- 1 pinch salt
- 1 tablespoon butter
- 1 teaspoon vanilla extract
- 1 teaspoon baking soda

Instructions

1. Grease a baking sheet, and set aside.
2. In a microwaveable bowl, combine peanuts, sugar, corn syrup, and salt. Microwave for 6 to 7 minutes or until bubbly and peanuts have browned. Stir in butter and vanilla and cook 2 to 3 minutes more.
3. Quickly stir in baking soda, until mixture turns foamy. Pour immediately onto greased baking sheet. Cool 15 minutes or until set.
4. Break into pieces, and store in an airtight container.

S'mores Cheesecake Dip

Ingredients

- 1 container (8 oz.) PHILADELPHIA Milk Chocolate Snack Delights
- ⅓ cup marshmallow crème
- Graham sticks, pretzels, or fruits of your choice

Instructions

1. Add cream cheese to a bowl and swirl marshmallow with a knife.
2. Serve with pretzels, fruit or graham sticks.

Vanilla Iced Coffee Pudding

SERVINGS: 15
PREP TIME: 20 min.
TOTAL TIME: 30 min.

Ingredients

- 1 pkg. (1oz) Sugar Free vanilla pudding mix
- ¾ cup skim milk
- 1 cup International Delight Vanilla Iced Coffee
- 16 oz. Light Cool Whip, thawed
- 2 oz. milk chocolate, chopped

Instructions

1. In a large mixing bowl whisk pudding mix with milk for 2 minutes. Whisk in the Iced Coffee. Fold in Cool Whip until completely blended.
2. Pour pudding into a large bowl, or individual serving dishes.
3. Top with chopped chocolate bar and allow to set for 30 minutes.
4. Store in refrigerator until ready to serve.

Cherry Vanilla Puppy Chow

SERVINGS: 8
PREP TIME: 10 min.
TOTAL TIME: 20 min.

Ingredients

- 8 cup rice Chex cereal
- 1 pkg. (16 oz.) Vanilla bark (almond candy coating)
- 1 pkg. (0.3 oz.) Sugar Free JELL-O cherry gelatin mix
- 1¾ cup powdered sugar
- sprinkles

Instructions

1. Place vanilla bark in a microwaveable dish and microwave for 1 minute. Stir, microwave an additional 30 seconds until creamy. Mix in cherry gelatin mix.
2. In a large bowl, mix together the cereal with melted chocolate. Stir until coated. Pour into a large gallon sized container with powdered sugar and shake well. Pour onto a large baking sheet with foil, until set. Add sprinkles.

Ice Cream Treasures

SERVINGS: 16
PREP/TOTAL TIME: 20 min. + refrigeration

Ingredients

- 1 ½ cups (6 oz.) chocolate-covered English toffee candy bars, crushed
- 8 cups vanilla reduced-fat ice cream, softened
- 4 cups crispy rice cereal squares, crushed (such as Rice Chex)
- 2 cups whole-grain toasted oat cereal (such as Cheerios)
- ⅔ cup packed dark brown sugar
- ⅓ cup slivered almonds, toasted
- ⅓ cup flaked sweetened coconut, toasted
- 2 tablespoons butter, melted

Instructions

1. Stir crushed candy into ice cream. Cover and freeze until ready to use.
2. Combine cereals, brown sugar, and remaining ingredients in a large bowl, stirring until well blended. Press half of cereal mixture in bottom of a 13 x 9-inch baking pan.
3. Let ice cream stand at room temperature 20 minutes or until soft. Spread softened ice cream mixture over cereal mixture. Top evenly with remaining cereal mixture.
4. Cover and freeze 8 hours or overnight.

English Toffee

SERVINGS: 8
PREP TIME: 10 min.
TOTAL TIME: 20 hours

Ingredients

- 1 cup butter
- 1 cup sugar
- 3 tablespoons water
- ⅛ teaspoon salt (do not use if you use salted butter)
- 1½ tablespoons light corn syrup
- 1 teaspoon vanilla extract
- ¾ cup chocolate chips
- chopped nuts (optional)

Instructions

1. Melt butter in a heavy-bottom sauce pan over medium-low heat. Add sugar, water, and salt. Stir well to incorporate. Bring to a boil and add corn syrup. While stirring, use a wet pastry brush to wash down the sides of the pan to dissolve any undissolved sugar crystals. Continue boiling and stirring. Remove from heat and add the vanilla extract.
2. Stir to combine and pour into a well-buttered cookie sheet or an 8×8 inch casserole dish. Do not scrape the sides of the pan. Use a rubber scraper and spread out to desired thickness. Drop the chocolate chips onto the hot toffee and spread out when melted, or melt the chocolate in the microwave and spread over the toffee. Sprinkle with chopped nuts, if desired.
3. Allow to set and break into chunks.

Cookies & Cream Melt-Aways

SERVINGS: 8
PREP/TIME: 10 min. + refrigeration

Ingredients

- 40 Oreos
- 1 cup unsalted butter, divided
- 3 cup powdered sugar
- 2 tablespoons milk
- 1 teaspoon vanilla

Instructions

1. With a food processor or blender, finely crush 30 Oreos.
2. Combine Oreo crumbs with ½ cup softened butter. Press into 9x9 inch pan to form crust.
3. Chill crust until firm.
4. Combine powdered sugar, ½ cup softened butter, milk, and vanilla in a medium mixing bowl. Blend on medium-high speed for 2-3 minutes.
5. Crush remaining 10 Oreos, leaving some larger pieces, and stir into powdered sugar mix. Spread over top of crust and keep refrigerated until ready to serve.

Muddy Buddies

SERVINGS: 12-15
PREP/TOTAL TIME: 10 min.

Ingredients

- 9 cups Chex cereal
- 1 cup semi-sweet chocolate chips
- ½ cup peanut butter
- ¼ cup margarine
- 1 teaspoon vanilla extract
- 1 ½ cup powdered sugar

Instructions

1. Pour cereal into large bowl and set aside.
2. Combine chocolate chips, peanut butter and margarine in 1-quart, microwave-safe bowl. Microwave at 100-percent power for 1 to 1 ½ minutes or until smooth, stirring after 1 minute. Stir in vanilla.
3. Pour chocolate sauce over cereal, stirring to evenly coat.
4. Pour cereal into large plastic bag. Add powdered sugar and shake to coat. Spread on waxed paper to cool.

Chocolate Peanut Butter Dessert

SERVINGS: 8
PREP/TOTAL TIME: 15 min. + refrigeration

Ingredients

- 20 Oreo cookies, divided
- 2 tablespoons butter, softened
- 1 package (8 oz.) cream cheese, softened
- ½ cup peanut butter
- 1½ cups confectioners' sugar, divided
- 1 carton (16 oz.) frozen whipped topping, thawed, divided
- 15-20 miniature peanut butter cups, chopped
- 1 cup cold milk
- 1 package (3.9 oz.) instant chocolate pudding mix

Instructions

1. Crush 16 cookies and toss with butter. Press into an ungreased 9-inch square dish and set aside.
2. In a large bowl, beat cream cheese, peanut butter and 1 cup confectioners' sugar until smooth.
3. Fold in half of the whipped topping and spread over crust.
4. Sprinkle with chopped peanut butter cups.
5. In a large bowl, beat milk, pudding mix and remaining confectioners' sugar on low speed for 2 minutes. Let stand a few minutes or until soft-set.
6. Fold in remaining whipped topping and spread over peanut butter cups.
7. Crush remaining cookies and sprinkle over the top.
8. Cover and chill for at least 3 hours.

Coconut Almond Chex Mix

SERVINGS: 12
PREP/TOTAL TIME: 15 min.

Ingredients

- 1 (14 oz.-17 oz.) box of Rice or Corn Chex cereal
- 7 oz. bag of sweetened coconut
- 5 oz. bag of almonds (about 1⅓ cup)
- 1½ cups sugar
- 1½ sticks (¾ cup) margarine or butter
- 1¼ cups light corn syrup
- Dash of salt

Instructions

1. Spray a very large bowl with non-stick cooking spray. Pour in the entire box of Chex cereal, coconut, and almonds. Mix together gently.
2. In a medium saucepan over high heat, mix the sugar, butter, light corn syrup, and dash of salt. Bring to a full boil, turn heat to medium, and cook for three minutes, constantly stirring. Pour over the cereal mix in the big bowl stirring evenly.
3. Spread cereal evenly on wax paper and let cool.
4. Place in a bowl and serve.

THANK YOU

Thank you for checking out my No-Bake Desserts Cookbook. I hope you enjoyed these recipes as much as I have. I am always looking for feedback on how to improve, so if you have any questions, suggestions, or comments please send me an email at susan.evans.author@gmail.com. Also, if you enjoyed the book would you consider leaving on honest review? As a new author, they help me out in a big way. Thanks again, and have fun cooking!

Other popular books by Susan Evans

Quick & Easy Vegan Desserts Cookbook:
Over 80 delicious recipes for cakes, cupcakes, brownies, cookies, fudge, pies, candy, and so much more!

Quick & Easy Microwave Meals:
Over 50 recipes for breakfast, snacks, meals and desserts

Quick & Easy Asian Vegetarian Cookbook:
Over 50 recipes for stir fries, rice, noodles, and appetizers

Vegetarian Mediterranean Cookbook:
Over 50 recipes for appetizers, salads, dips, and main dishes

The Vegetarian DASH Diet Cookbook:
Over 100 recipes for breakfast, lunch, dinner and sides!

The Complete Rice Cooker Meals Cookbook Bundle:
Over 100 recipes for breakfast, main dishes, soups, and desserts!

Vegetarian Slow Cooker Cookbook:
Over 75 recipes for meals, soups, stews, desserts, and sides

Halloween Cookbook:
80 Ghoulish recipes for appetizers, meals, drinks, and desserts

Printed in Great Britain
by Amazon